DOLPHINS

Jen Green

Grolier
an imprint of
SCHOLASTIC

www.scholastic.com/librarypublishing

Published 2009 by Grolier
An Imprint of Scholastic Library Publishing
Old Sherman Turnpike
Danbury, Connecticut 06816

For The Brown Reference Group
Project Editor: Jolyon Goddard
Picture Researchers: Clare Newman,
Sophie Mortimer
Designer: Sarah Williams
Managing Editor: Tim Harris

Volume ISBN-13: 978-0-7172-8064-3
Volume ISBN-10: 0-7172-8064-0

**Library of Congress
Cataloging-in-Publication Data**

Nature's children. Set 6.
   p. cm.
  Includes index.
  ISBN-13: 978-0-7172-8085-8
  ISBN-10: 0-7172-8085-3
  I. Animals--Encyclopedias, Juvenile. I.
Grolier (Firm)
  QL49.N387 2009
  590.3--dc22
                        2008014675

Printed and bound in China

PICTURE CREDITS

Front Cover: **Shutterstock**: Tom Hirtreiter.

Back Cover: **Shutterstock**: Tom C. Amon,
Ferenc Cegledi, Kristian Sekulic, Jenny
Solomon.

Corbis: Stephen Frink 26, 34, Jeffrey L.
Rotman 22, 33, 46; **Imagebank**: Paolo Curto
14, Images Unlimited 18, Gerard Mathieu 9;
Thomas Schmitt 17, 38, Joseph van Os 10;
NHPA: A.N.T. Photo Library 6, 13, 30–31,
37, 42, Henry Ausloos 45 Norbert Wu 25;
Shutterstock: Lars Christensen 4, Ulises
Sepúlveda Déniz 5, Four Oaks 2–3, Kristian
Sekulic 21. **Werner Forman Archive**: 41.

Contents

FACT FILE: Dolphins

Class	Mammals (Mammalia)
Order	Whales (Cetacea)
Families	Dolphins (Delphinoidea) and river dolphins (Lipotidae, Iniidae, Platanistidae, and Pontoporiidae)
Genera	24 genera
Species	There at least 36 species of oceanic dolphins and four species of river dolphins
World distribution	Seas and oceans worldwide, except in the polar regions; river dolphins are found in the Amazon, Ganges, Indus, and Yangtze
Habitat	Open oceans, coastal waters, or great rivers
Distinctive physical characteristics	Sleek, streamlined body; pointed teeth; muscular tail ending in twin flukes; a single blowhole on top of the head
Habits	Dolphins live in schools, usually of 20 to 100 animals; males and females often form separate groups within the school
Diet	Fish, squid, and shellfish

Introduction

Dolphins are skillful animals. These fish-shaped **mammals** are well suited to their watery home. They can swim fast when hunting for food. They have a special sense to "see" their **prey** in murky water, and they can even talk to one another. Dolphins live in all the oceans of the world. A few types of dolphins even live in freshwater rivers. However, one of these dolphins—the Yangtze river dolphin—may now be **extinct**.

Dolphins are descended from land animals that returned to live in water about 50 million years ago.

5

Dolphins often
follow ships.

6

Friendly Faces

A dolphin's face always looks as though it is smiling, and a dolphin always wants to play. Dolphins are not afraid of people and seem to like human company.

In stories and television shows, dolphins are often shown helping during a crisis, such as rescuing people in trouble. They always seem to know when there is danger at sea. Their arrival usually means that help is on the way. These stories are often based on true incidents when real dolphins have helped and made friends with humans.

What Are Dolphins?

Which is more like a dolphin, a fish or a human?
You may be surprised to hear that, in many ways,
the answer is a human. A dolphin looks a lot
like a fish and spends its life in water. Dolphins,
however, are mammals—warm-blooded animals
like humans. A dolphin mother gives birth to
her baby and feeds it milk, just like human
mothers do. A dolphin even has a bellybutton
like a human's!

Of course, dolphins are not very closely
related to people. They are types of whales.
The whale family is divided into two groups:
whales with teeth and whales that have large,
horny plates like sieves instead of teeth. Like
porpoises, dolphins belong to the group of
whales with teeth.

"Give me a fish!"
This bottlenose
dolphin shows off
its pointed teeth.

Dolphins are a common sight in many of the world's oceans.

Dolphin Territory

Have you been lucky enough to see a dolphin in the wild? Most people have probably seen living dolphins only in a **dolphinarium**. All the same, dolphins are probably found in the sea nearest you. Dolphins live in seas and oceans all over the world, except in the very cold waters of the Arctic and Antarctic oceans.

About 40 different **species** of dolphins are found worldwide. Some kinds stick to shallow waters close to shore. Others swim far out to sea and have the whole ocean for their playground. Most dolphins live in salty seawater, but a few kinds live in freshwater. They are found in some of the world's great rivers, including the Amazon—the longest river in the world. A few kinds of dolphins, such as the tucuxi (TOO-KOO-SHEE) from South America, can be found both in rivers and in the sea.

Sleek Shapes

A dolphin's shape is just right for life in the ocean. Its long, sleek body is shaped like a torpedo, so it glides easily through the water. Dolphins have two **flippers**, or chest **fins**, shaped like paddles. Most kinds have a triangular fin on their back, like a shark. Dolphins are propelled by a strong tail that ends in two wide, flat fins called **flukes**.

The Heaviside's dolphin is the smallest member of the family, growing to 4 feet (1.2 m) long. Most dolphins, however, are much longer. A male bottlenose dolphin can grow to 12 feet (3.6 m) in length and weigh up to 650 pounds (300 kg). Placed on gigantic weighing scales, it would outweigh three adult men on the other side. Female dolphins are often a little smaller than males.

Most people do not think of the orca, or killer whale, as a dolphin, but it is in fact the biggest member of the dolphin family. Males can grow to 23 feet (7 m) long and weigh 7 tons (7 tonnes). This black-and-white giant often eats its smaller relatives!

The sleek body shape of these spotted dolphins helps them move quickly and easily through the water.

The thick layer of blubber beneath a dolphin's skin helps keep the animal warm in the water.

Keeping Warm

In water, a human body loses heat 25 times
faster than in air. How do dolphins, which
are also warm-blooded animals, keep warm in
the water all day long? If you had a chance to
stroke a dolphin, it would feel soft and velvety.
Underneath the dolphin's skin is a thick layer
of fat, called **blubber**. This layer keeps cold out
and the dolphin's body heat in, like the rubber
wet suit of a sea diver. The blubber also acts as
an emergency food store. The animal can live
off this fatty layer when food is scarce.

Swift Swimmers

A dolphin moves through the water powered by its muscular tail. Unlike a fish, which swishes its tail from side to side, a dolphin sweeps its tail flukes up and down. Both the upstroke and the downstroke provide pushing power, driving the animal through the water. The flippers are only used for steering.

Dolphins are expert swimmers. They can race along at 34 miles (55 km) per hour, which is as fast as a powerboat. These bursts of speed can only be kept up for a short distance. Dolphins use these bursts of speed to catch their food and to escape from enemies if they have to.

Dolphins are graceful as well as speedy in the water. They can turn cartwheels like circus acrobats, swim upside down, and even balance on their tail.

When they are swimming fast, dolphins often leap into the air to take a breath.

Dolphins can dive as deep as 1,000 feet (305 m) down into the sea in search of food.

Big Breaths

A dolphin breathes through its single nostril, called a **blowhole**. The blowhole is found on top of its head, so the dolphin does not have to lift its face out of the water to breathe. The blowhole closes tight when the dolphin dives, so water cannot get in. When it surfaces, the blowhole opens again. The dolphin snorts out the stale air in its **lungs** and breathes in a fresh supply.

Dolphins can hold their breath underwater for 15 minutes or more. They are able to do that because their muscles contain a substance called **myoglobin**. Myoglobin stores oxygen and slowly releases it when the dolphin dives underwater. However, like all mammals, dolphins must eventually return to the surface to breathe in fresh oxygen from the air.

Jump for Joy

Dolphins can do many tricks when swimming. They can swim so fast that they leap clear out of the water and fly through the air before diving in again.

When a dolphin leaps out of the water, it is called **breaching**. It breaches partly so it can take a breath without slowing down. But dolphins leap much higher than they need to for breathing alone. Young dolphins leap for fun. Older dolphins sometimes breach to attract attention and warn others of danger.

Dolphins can leap more than 20 feet (6 m) into the air. The faster a dolphin swims, the higher it can jump. By measuring the height of their highest jumps, scientists can work out their top speeds.

A dolphin's blowhole is clearly visible as it breaches.

A bottlenose
dolphin feeds
on an octopus
in the Red Sea.

On the Menu

If you invited a dolphin to lunch, what would you serve? A dolphin would relish a plate of octopus or squid as a first course. For your entrée you should serve plenty of fish. Dolphins eat a variety of small fish, including mackerel, herring, and sardines. To finish off, a dolphin would enjoy a tasty dish of eels. If it got hungry later on, it would love a little snack of anchovies or shrimps.

Dolphins are big eaters and usually stick to waters where they can find a lot of of their favorite prey. An adult dolphin needs to eat as much as 20 pounds (9 kg) of fish a day to feel full. That's more fish than some humans eat in a year! Some dolphins swim hundreds of miles each year to visit hunting grounds where fish are plentiful.

A Toothy Grin

Some dolphins have a smooth, rounded head and can be confused with porpoises—their smaller, less acrobatic relatives. Most, however, are easily identified by their long, pointed nose, called a **beak**. At the water's surface, dolphins often open their mouth, showing off their sharp teeth. A river dolphin's long beak is lined with more than 100 pointy teeth. It looks like it belongs to a crocodile!

Dolphins swallow their food whole, so they do not need their teeth for chewing. Instead, the teeth are used to keep a tight grip on slippery fish as they try to wriggle away. Then, with one slurp of its tongue, the dolphin gulps down the tasty morsels it has caught.

Not all dolphins are well behaved at feeding time. To get in the best position to catch fish, males sometimes jostle females and young out of the way.

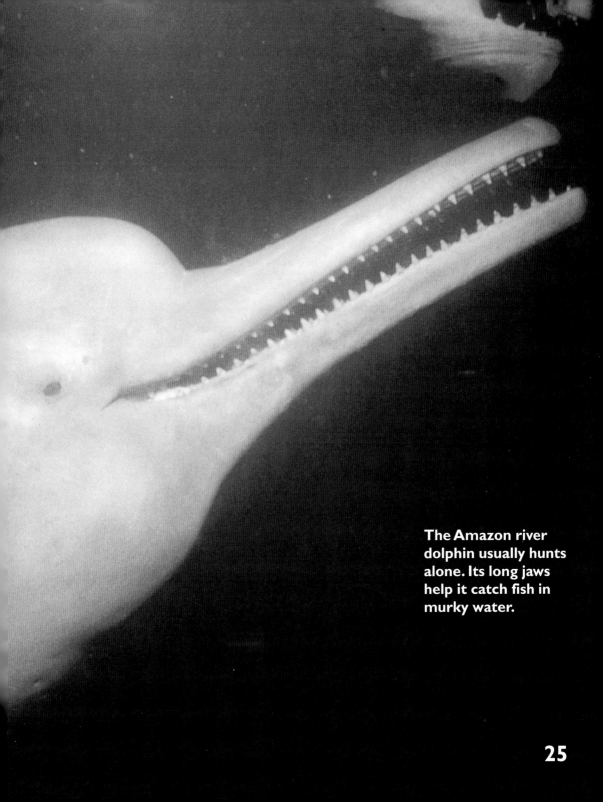

The Amazon river dolphin usually hunts alone. Its long jaws help it catch fish in murky water.

This pair of dolphins
pushes and shoves
each other to see
which is stronger.

Schooltime

How would you like to spend all of your time in school? A dolphin does, because the group it lives in is called a **school**. Just as people describe a herd of cattle or a flock of birds, they talk about a school of dolphins. Dolphin schools usually contain 20 to 100 animals, but some big schools have up to 1,000 members. A dolphin school is like a big, happy family, with brothers, sisters, uncles, aunts, and cousins all living together. Some teaching does go on in the school—young dolphins learn the skills they need to survive from the older animals.

Dolphins usually get along well with other members of their school. They are affectionate creatures and spend a lot of time greeting and touching one another. All families argue sometimes, however, and dolphins are no exception. The arguments are usually about which dolphin is in charge. Squabbling dolphins slap the water and squawk at one another. Most differences can be sorted out without anyone getting hurt.

Dolphin Chorus

Dolphins are very good singers, but most of the notes they sing are too high-pitched for humans to hear. They can make a lot of different noises, too, from clicks, whistles, and squeaks to groans like creaky doors. They produce the noises with little air sacs underneath their blowhole.

Dolphins click and squeak all the time. Scientists do not yet understand what all their noises mean, but they do know that each dolphin has its own special whistle. In the same way that a person has a unique voice, every dolphin has a signature tune. All the dolphins in a school can identify one another by their whistle.

Amazing Echoes

If you were a hungry dolphin, how would you track down your next meal? Your eyes would not be much help in the ocean because even in the clearest water it is hard to see very far. Swimming in murky water would be like walking through a thick mist or fog. So instead of relying on sight, dolphins use another, very special skill when they go hunting. Each dolphin produces a stream of clicking sounds. The sounds spread out through the water, and when they reach a fish, they echo back. The dolphin hears the echoes and can tell how large the fish is and which way to swim to catch it.

This amazing ability is called **echolocation**. It works just as well in the dark as it does in daylight, so some dolphins hunt at night and rest during the day.

A pair of spotted dolphins rises to the water's surface to breathe.

Teamwork

Dolphins work in a team when they are hunting.
Good timing is very important, so dolphins
all move together. The whole school comes
to the surface to take a breath and then dives
down again.

On a hunt, dolphins keep in close touch,
calling to one another with clicks and whistles.
The different sounds may mean, "Keep
together" or "I'm over here." Most types of
dolphins spread out in a long line to look
for food. When they find a **shoal** of fish,
they surround it in a big circle, diving and
splashing to herd their prey close together.
Once the fish are tightly packed, the dolphins
all dive into the middle to eat their fill.

After herding the fish together, the dolphin dives in for an easy meal.

A baby Atlantic spotted dolphin is protected by the adults swimming on each side of it.

34

Safety in Numbers

Dolphins look after one another. Members of the school all work together to make sure everyone is safe. In a big school, mothers and their young swim near the middle of the group. The dolphins on the outside protect the little ones from harm.

There are no hiding places in the open oceans. When a dolphin gets tired, it can't just curl up under the covers and go to sleep. It must stay alert, looking out for danger, and keep coming to the surface to breathe. Still dolphins need their rest. They get around the problem by having only half of their brain asleep at a time—that way they can keep one eye open to watch for enemies.

To the Rescue

Dolphins know that when danger threatens, the other members of their school will be there to help. Sailors have seen dolphins work together to defend an injured friend against a shark or orca. Dolphins will even attack a shark to protect their young, ramming it with their bodies to drive it away.

If a dolphin is wounded, the other members of its school answer its call and offer help. They support the injured animal with their bodies and lift it to the surface from time to time so it can breathe. They stay close and guard their friend until he or she is better.

If a dolphin spots danger, it blows a cloud of bubbles to warn the rest of the school.

At Monkey Mia, in Western Australia, a school of wild dolphins comes to the beach and plays with visitors.

Dolphins at Play

Dolphins love to have fun and are very friendly toward humans. They enjoy swimming alongside boats. One of their favorite games is to surf the bow waves that the front of the boat makes. Dolphins are especially fond of children, probably because they are small and gentle. They seem to be as curious about humans as humans are about them.

Dolphins that do not live in a school particularly seek out human company. Some return to the same place again and again to make friends and play with the people who swim out to meet them. These wild dolphins, called "friendlies," often become local celebrities, and people come from far and wide to see them. If you visited the western coast of Ireland and went swimming at Dingle Bay, you might meet a friendly dolphin called Fungi, which lives nearby and comes visiting nearly every day.

Trusty Friends

Dolphins do not just help their own kind—there are many stories about them helping people, too. Even the ancient Greeks, more than 2,000 years ago, knew of dolphins that made friends with humans and saved them from danger. Dolphins have been known to defend swimmers against shark attacks. In the Pacific Ocean during World War II (1939–1945), dolphins rescued airmen who had baled out of their planes and were drifting in life rafts. The dolphins gently pushed the little rafts to the shore with their bodies.

In some parts of West Africa, dolphins even help local people catch fish. When the fishermen spot a shoal of fish, they beat the water with sticks to call the dolphins. The dolphins arrive to drive the fish into the waiting nets and share the catch.

This ancient Greek vase shows a soldier riding to war on the back of a friendly dolphin.

A dusky dolphin balances on its tail.

Smart Students

Dolphins are extremely clever. In research centers, scientists have set up tests to find out just how smart they are. Dolphins learn new, difficult tasks quickly and can even tell one another how to do them. In one test, a dolphin told its neighbor in a different tank how to get food by pressing a paddle. Dolphins' echolocation is very sensitive, too. A dolphin can tell the difference between two balls of slightly different sizes even when wearing a blindfold.

Scientists try to work out dolphins' language and guess the meaning of the different sounds they make. However, it is hard for humans to understand how dolphins' minds work because the watery world they live in is so different from our world.

Expecting a Baby

Dolphins have a breeding season. During this time, male dolphins fight over which one gets to mate with the females. The time of the breeding season varies among different types of dolphins. For example, bottlenose dolphins mate in March and April. A baby dolphin is ready to be born 10 to 12 months after mating. About five months before it is due, the mother-to-be returns to her mother's group. In the group, there are several females that have given birth themselves and can help her have the baby.

This small band of females finds a quiet, shallow bay where fish are plentiful. As the baby's birth gets closer, the mother-to-be exercises and stretches her body, getting ready for the big day ahead. Usually only one baby is born, although sometimes there are twins. Dolphins live to about the age of 30, and females usually have eight babies—one every two or three years—during their lifetime.

Female bottlenose dolphins, such as these two in the Red Sea, stick close together when it's almost time for them to give birth.

This dolphin baby is only a few days old, but already it is able to keep up with its mother.

A Baby Is Born

Unlike other mammals, baby whales and dolphins are usually born tail-first. The baby's tail is often exposed during the period leading up to birth, called **labor**, which can last up to six hours. The actual birth happens quickly. The mother's friends encourage her during the birth and sometimes support her body. At last the baby is out. All that cold water must be a shock!

The baby does not float at first, because it has no air in its lungs. Quickly, the mother carries it to the water's surface on her back. The baby's blowhole opens, and it takes its first breath of air.

A young dolphin is called a **calf**. A newborn calf weighs about 35 pounds (16 kg). At first, its fins and tail flukes are soft and rubbery. They harden after a few days, helping the calf swim more easily.

Early Days

During the first few days, the baby learns how to **suckle** its mother's milk. It must take a big breath and dive down underneath her body to find her **teats**. After it has **nursed**, the baby pops back up again to breathe and rest.

Dolphin milk is very rich, and the calf grows quickly. After only two months, it is twice the weight it was when it was born. It swims with its mother and rides on the wave she makes as she glides through the water. After four months, the calf is bold enough to start exploring. But it is always ready to dash back to the safety of its mother's side. The calf begins to eat fish, but it still drinks its mother's milk for another year. It will be several years before the young dolphin is grown-up enough to take its place as an adult in the school.

Words to Know

Beak	The long nose of a dolphin.
Blowhole	The opening on top of a dolphin's head that acts as a nostril.
Blubber	A layer of fat beneath the dolphin's skin that keeps it warm in water.
Breaching	Leaping out of the water.
Calf	A young dolphin.
Dolphinarium	An aquarium or large tank where dolphins are kept on display.
Echolocation	A sound sense that dolphins use to find objects such as fish in the water.
Extinct	When all of a kind of animal have died out and are gone forever.
Fins	Flat parts of a dolphin's body. Fins are used for balance, swimming, or steering.
Flippers	Chest fins of a seal or dolphin.
Flukes	The two wide, flat parts that form a dolphin's tail.

49

Labor	The early stages of giving birth. Labor may last from 30 minutes to six hours in dolphins.
Lungs	The organs used for breathing.
Mammals	Warm-blooded animals that have a backbone. Female mammals feed milk to their young.
Myoglobin	A chemical in muscles that stores oxygen. The oxygen is used up when a dolphin holds its breath during diving.
Nursed	Drank its mother's milk.
Prey	Animals that other animals hunt.
School	A group of dolphins.
Shoal	Large group of fish swimming together.
Species	The scientific word for animals of the same type that breed together.
Suckle	To nurse, or drink its mother's milk.
Teats	The parts of a female mammal's body that release milk.

Find Out More

Books

Baglio, B. M. *Dolphin in the Deep*. Animal Ark Series. New York: Scholastic, 2001.

Nicklin, F., and L. Nicklin. *Face to Face with Dolphins*. Face to Face with Animals. Washington D.C.: National Geographic Children's Books, 2007.

Web sites

Dolphins at Enchanted Learning
www.enchantedlearning.com/themes/dolphins.shtml
Plenty of facts and pictures of dolphins.

The Secret Language of Dolphins
kids.nationalgeographic.com/Stories/AnimalsNature/
Dolphin-language
Learn about how dolphins communicate.

Index